America's Amazing State Capitols:
A Journal and Guide for Students

Copyright ©2018 by Ellen Stanton

All rights reserved

No part of this book may be used or reproduced in any manner
without written permission except in the case of brief quotations
embodied in critical articles and reviews.

Resources:
National Conference of State Legislatures
The Council of State Governments (The Book of the States, 2017)
Official State Capitol websites.

Cover and Interior Design: Kathleen Munroe, Starr Design, www.starrdesign.biz
Illustrations: Jeff Mlady & Kathleen Munroe

Type is set in Museo and Recherche

ISBN: 978-0-692-15388-8

Printed in the United States of America

Introduction

We the people are able visit our statehouses or capitols to view the buildings and learn more about our state government. This is important because as Americans we celebrate open government. We can see where and how our government works.

Use this book as you explore your capitol and discover interesting facts about your state. Every state is unique and so, too, is each state capitol. State capitols feature impressive architecture, art, and history. This is your guide for a fun and exciting visit to your state capitol!

Every state in the United States of America has a capital city. The capital is the political center of a state because all three branches of state government meet there. The three branches are the legislative (makes the laws), executive (carries out the laws) and judicial (interprets the laws). Only one city can be the official capital of a state. United States territories have capitals as well. *Check out the map of the United States and look for each capital city.*

Notes

What is the origin of your capital city's name?

Some capital cities are named after cities in Great Britain; a few are American Indian names, and many are named after people. Four state capitals are named after Presidents; can you find them?

Within each capital city is a building that is called the state capitol, statehouse, or legislative hall. The state capitol symbolizes our political system, called a representative democracy. The people rule by electing representatives; each elected person acts for many citizens. The statehouse also represents the state and the pride that people feel as residents. The rooms (or chambers) where the legislature meets are located in the capitol or in a legislative hall. In most states the governor's office is located in the capitol as well. The governor leads the executive branch of state government. The state supreme court is located within the capitol in twelve states.

Notes

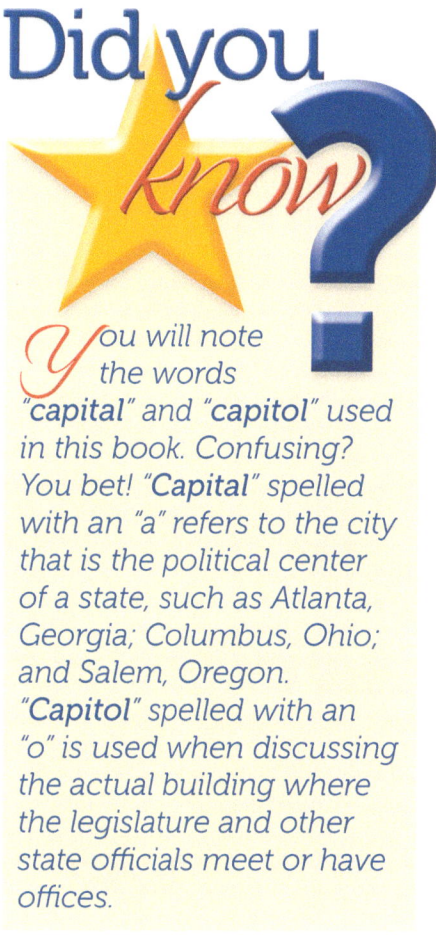

Did you know?

*You will note the words "**capital**" and "**capitol**" used in this book. Confusing? You bet! "**Capital**" spelled with an "a" refers to the city that is the political center of a state, such as Atlanta, Georgia; Columbus, Ohio; and Salem, Oregon. "**Capitol**" spelled with an "o" is used when discussing the actual building where the legislature and other state officials meet or have offices.*

Today the United States consists of 50 states. When we first became a nation in 1776 by declaring our independence, we were a nation of 13 states. Those states were located along the east coast. How did other states join the nation? People began moving west to obtain land and seek their fortune. The new settlers organized into territories that later became states through federal legislation. Some states, like Maine and Texas, became part of the U.S. without ever being territories.

Notes

In what year did your state become part of the union?

What is the story of its becoming a state?

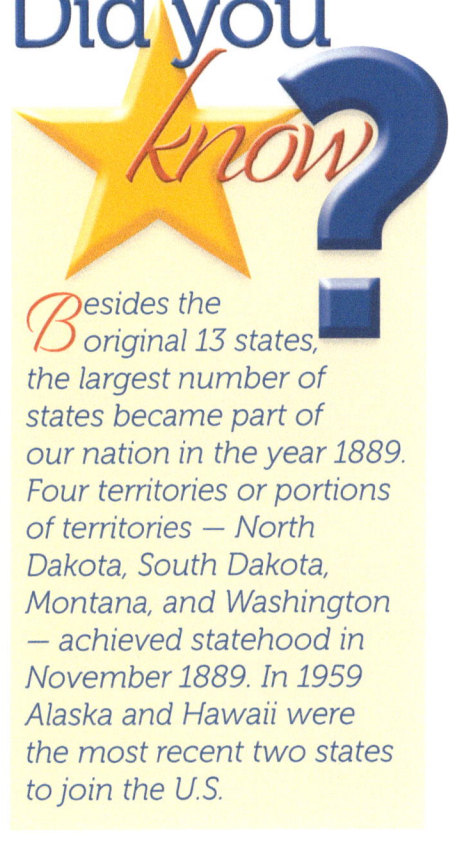

Did you know?

Besides the original 13 states, the largest number of states became part of our nation in the year 1889. Four territories or portions of territories — North Dakota, South Dakota, Montana, and Washington — achieved statehood in November 1889. In 1959 Alaska and Hawaii were the most recent two states to join the U.S.

Once a new state was approved, the state had to decide on a capital city. Often more than one city wanted to be the capital of the state. Some states, as they gained more citizens, changed their capital from one city to another. Sometimes the state capital is the city with the largest population or located in a convenient place, but that is not always the case.

Considerations for State Capital

- ☑ Central location
- ☐ Population
- ☑ Access to roads
- ☑ Convenient to rivers
- ☑ Nearby railroads
- ☑ Citizen approval and support

Notes

What city is the capital of your state?

Why was it chosen?

Did your state have a different capital in the past?

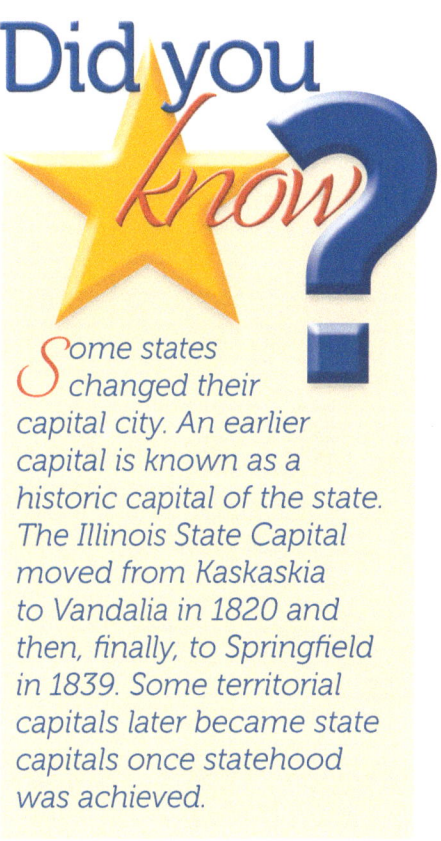

Did you know?

Some states changed their capital city. An earlier capital is known as a historic capital of the state. The Illinois State Capital moved from Kaskaskia to Vandalia in 1820 and then, finally, to Springfield in 1839. Some territorial capitals later became state capitals once statehood was achieved.

Citizens want their capitols to be beautiful and impressive buildings. The designers select the finest materials, workmanship, and art to honor their state. Usually a group of people is selected to be in charge of construction.

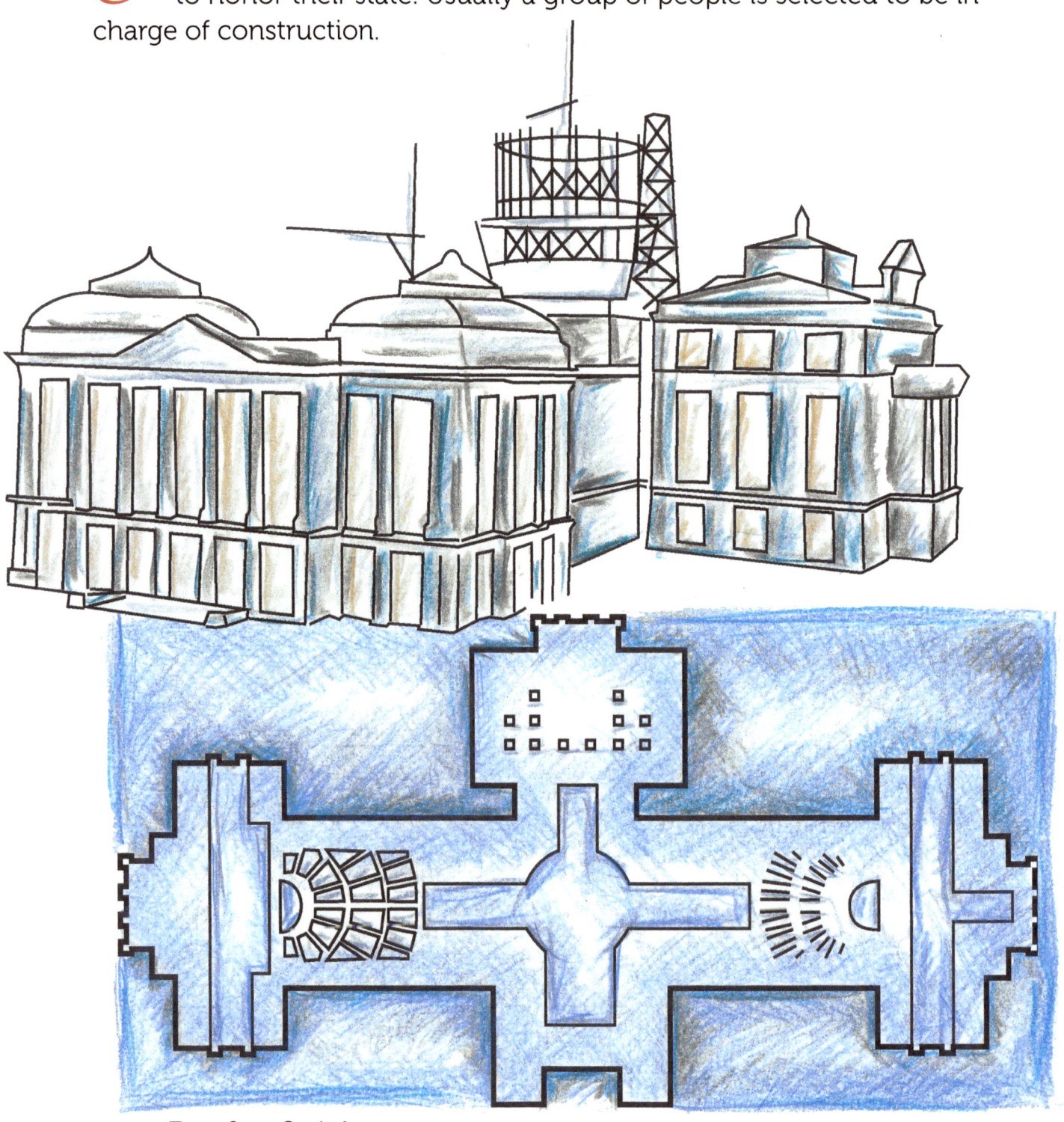

Texas State Capitol

Notes

What do you think is important to consider when planning a capitol building? Think about the size of the building, use and organization of the rooms, construction material, design, and cost.

*Where would you look for ideas? How would you make the building special for **your** state?*

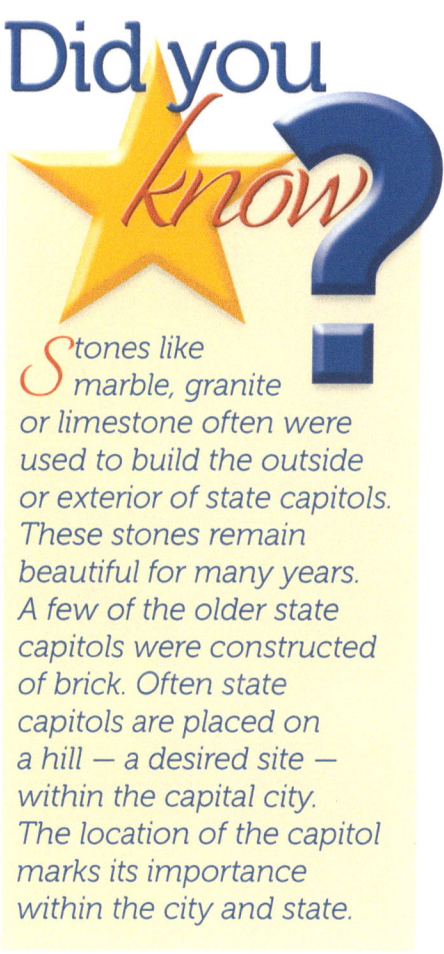

Did you know?

Stones like marble, granite or limestone often were used to build the outside or exterior of state capitols. These stones remain beautiful for many years. A few of the older state capitols were constructed of brick. Often state capitols are placed on a hill — a desired site — within the capital city. The location of the capitol marks its importance within the city and state.

The design or architecture of a capitol building sends a message. Sometimes the design reminds us of ancient Greece or Rome. We borrowed ideas about democracy ("the people rule") and representation from those cultures. Some capitols were intentionally designed to look like the U.S. Capitol in Washington, D.C. Other designs suggest modern ideas or something unique to the state. Much thought is put into the design of state capitols.

Wisconsin State Capitol

Did you know?

The New Mexico State Capitol in Santa Fe is the only round capitol found in the U.S. When seen from above, the design looks like the Zia Sun Symbol. The Hawaii State Capitol in Honolulu includes columns that look like palm trees. A pool surrounding the building represents the Pacific Ocean. The legislative rooms are cone-shaped, symbolizing the volcanoes that formed the Hawaiian Islands.

Notes

How would you describe your state capitol? Between which years was it built?

Nebraska State Capitol

Some state capitols are similar to other capitols. Others are unique in appearance. Thomas Jefferson is the most famous architect of a state capitol. In 1785 the future third president of United States, along with French architect Charles-Louis Clerisseau, designed the Virginia Capitol. He based his design on an ancient Roman temple located in France. Elijah E. Myers designed three state capitols (Michigan, Texas, and Colorado)!

Virginia State Capitol

Colorado State Capitol

Notes

Who designed your state capitol? What other buildings did that architect design?

Did you know?

William Strickland was the architect of the Tennessee State Capitol. He died in 1854 during its construction and is buried in a tomb in the capitol! He was a noted architect who designed several important buildings. The graves of the 11th U.S. President, James Polk, and his wife are found on the Tennessee State Capitol grounds. President Polk also was a governor of Tennessee.

Buildings are altered or changed over time. The oldest state capitol in continuous use is the Maryland State Capitol. Why would changes be made to a capitol? Sometimes states build additions onto their capitol. A few states moved the legislature out of the "old" capitol into a "new" legislative building. Recently, some states have restored their capitol to look as it did when it was new.

Massachusetts State Capitol

Notes

Have changes been made to your state capitol? Does it still look the same way it did when it was constructed?

Six additions have been added to the original 1792 New Jersey State Capitol. Older state capitol buildings within the current capital city are found in several states, including Arizona, Delaware, Florida, Kentucky, and Louisiana. Today, these buildings are state history museums. In these states, the legislature, supreme court, and governor's office are located in newer buildings.

Many state capitols have domes. A dome is a rounded roof, much like the upper half of a circle or sphere. The U.S. Capitol dome is one of the most famous domes in the world. Domes can be seen from a distance and indicate an important building. Domes are beautiful both from outside and inside the building. Often domes are topped with sculptures.

Look at the drawings below of domes found on the Idaho and Alabama state capitols.
What features are found on the tops of the dome?

Idaho State Capitol

Alabama State Capitol

Notes

Did you know?

Some state capitols have large gold domes, stone domes, or metal domes. Others are topped with small domes or cupolas (a small structure on top of a roof). The New York State Capitol is unusual in that it does not have a central roof feature such as a dome or cupola. The Connecticut State Capitol has a gold dome, cupola, and pointed arches and roofs. It looks like a castle!

Art and important symbols are found within state capitols. Famous citizens are honored in paintings, sculptures, and stained glass windows. States adopt mottos that express a state's beliefs or ideals. California's state motto is "Eureka" (a Greek word) and means "I have found it." It is believed that the motto refers to the discovery of gold in California.

Notes

Who is your favorite person from the past celebrated in your state capitol?

What symbols can you find in your state capitol? Look for flags, state seals, and state birds, trees, and flowers.

List symbols that you find.

Draw in the space below one of your state symbols.

Did you know?

More than 20 states call a type of butterfly their state insect. Ladybugs are popular state insects as well. Horses are favorite state animals, as are sea mammals such as whales and dolphins.

Why do we have three branches of government? The nation's founders thought it was important for the three branches to balance one another. Each branch of government has a different purpose. When government is balanced, no single branch has too much power.

The Tenth Amendment of the United States Constitution states that power not given to the federal government is reserved for the states. *What does that mean?*

Answer: The federal government has only those powers specifically stated in the U.S. Constitution. Any power not listed is granted to the states or the people.

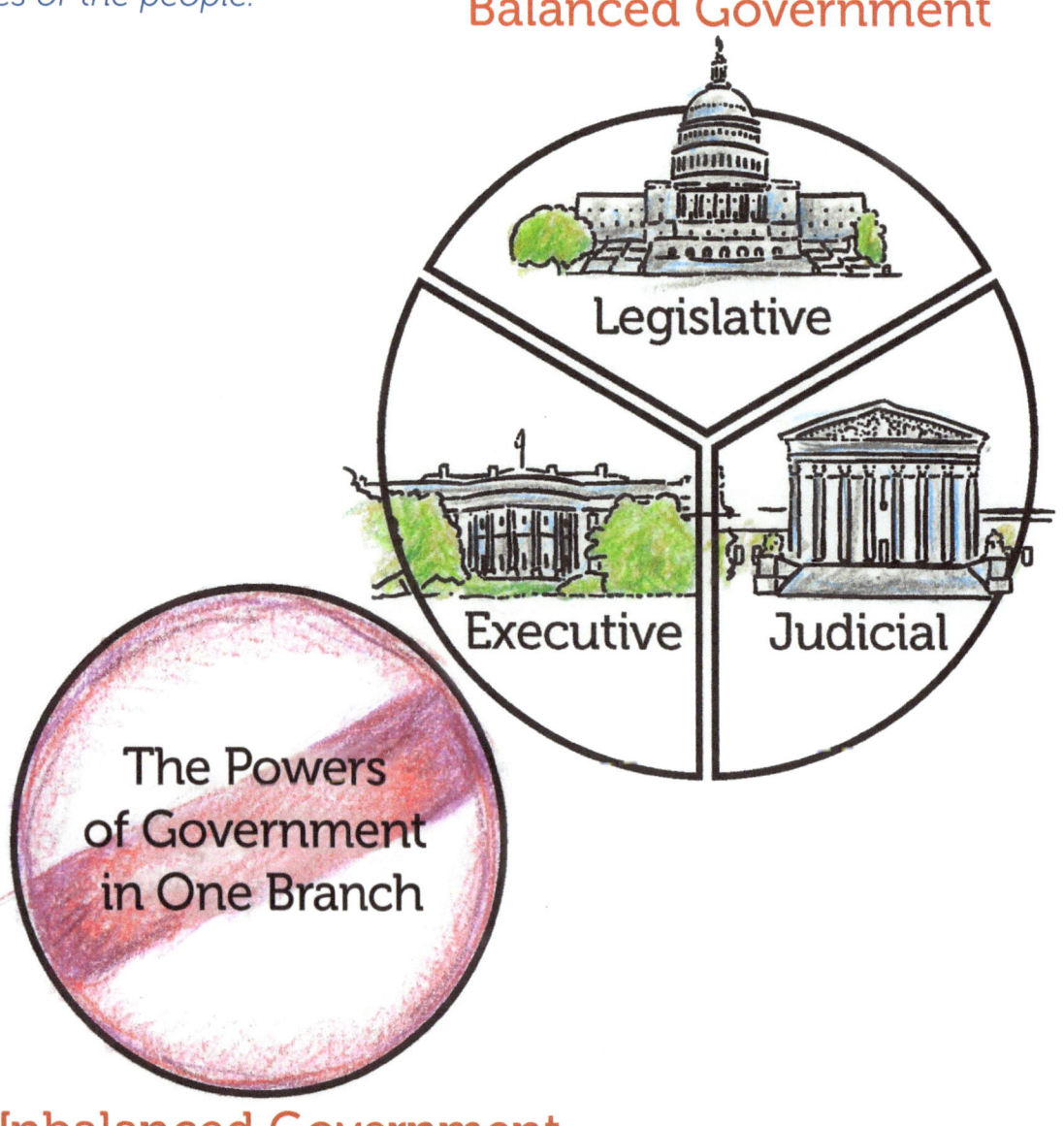

Balanced Government

Legislative

Executive   Judicial

The Powers of Government in One Branch

Unbalanced Government

Notes

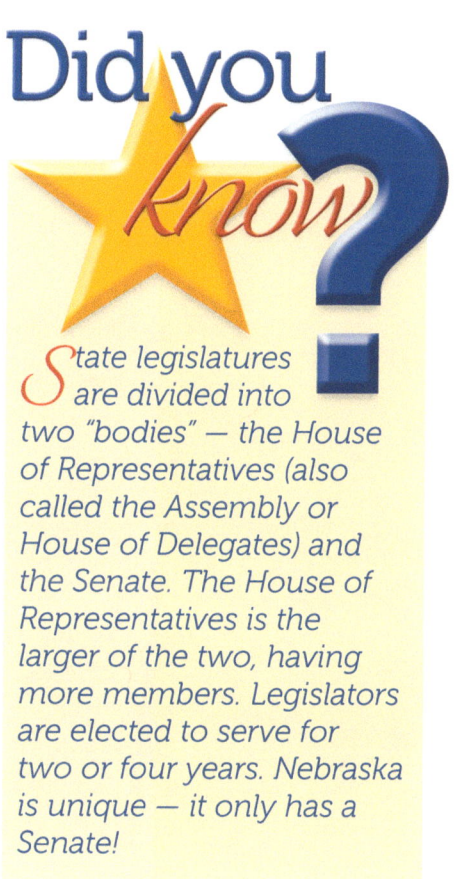

Did you know?

State legislatures are divided into two "bodies" — the House of Representatives (also called the Assembly or House of Delegates) and the Senate. The House of Representatives is the larger of the two, having more members. Legislators are elected to serve for two or four years. Nebraska is unique — it only has a Senate!

Each state decides how it will govern by writing a constitution. States determine when and how often the legislature meets, the number of members, and the length of terms of office. The number of years a representative is elected is called a term of office. States decide how the executive branch (governor) and judicial branch (judges) are organized. States make changes to their constitutions called amendments.

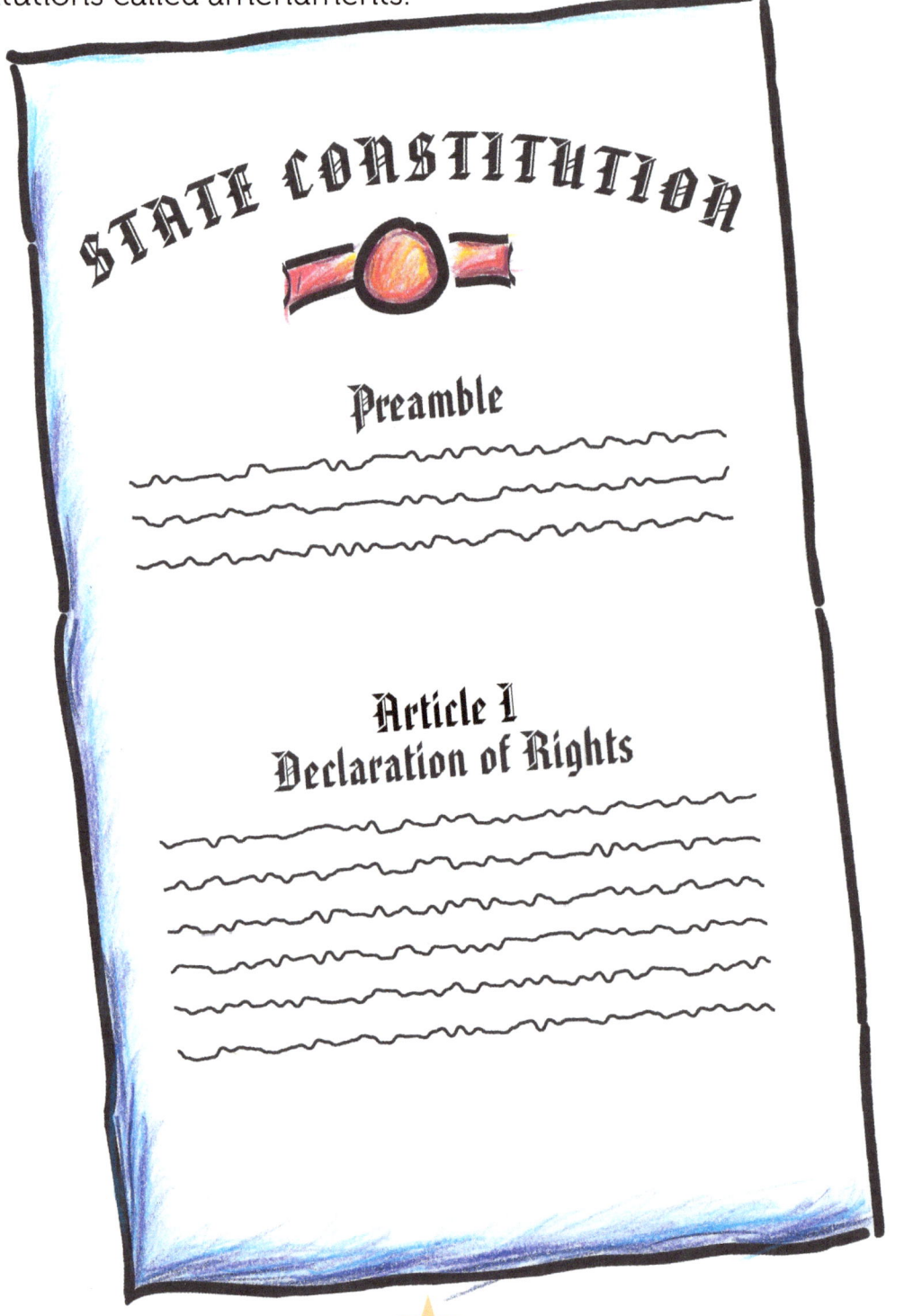

Notes

Find out how your state government is organized by discovering information on your state government website.

Did you know?

The number of legislators varies in each state. Since Nebraska has just a Senate, the state has a total of 49 legislators. Alaska has the second lowest number with 60 legislators. The greatest numbers of legislators serve in New Hampshire. The New Hampshire House of Representatives has 400 members and their Senate has 24 members.

What laws are passed by states? Do they matter to you? Absolutely! States pass laws regarding the number of days per year students spend in school, money approved for K-12 education and state universities, road and public safety issues, and minimum wage and work rules.

Notes

Ask a librarian to help you look up laws recently passed in your state.

Which laws do you find most interesting?

If you were elected to serve in the legislature, which ideas or bills would you support?

State legislatures are known by different names. The most common name is Legislature or State Legislature. Sometimes they are called the General Assembly or Legislative Assembly. Two states, Massachusetts and New Hampshire, call their legislature the General Court.

Americans often discuss U.S. presidential elections, but do we pay as much attention to state and local elections? Do you know the name of your mayor and governor? Who represents you in your state legislature? How many judges are on your state supreme court?

Notes

Research someone who works in your state government.

What is their job and why do they serve?

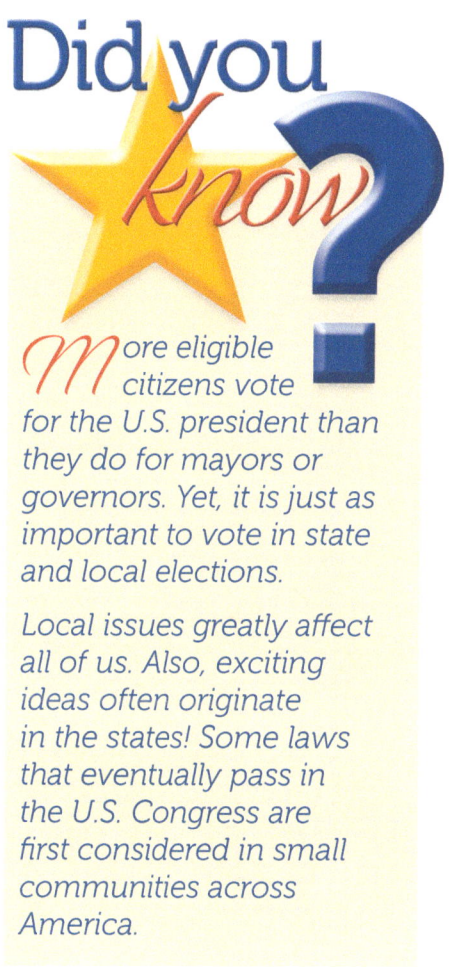

Did you know?

More eligible citizens vote for the U.S. president than they do for mayors or governors. Yet, it is just as important to vote in state and local elections.

Local issues greatly affect all of us. Also, exciting ideas often originate in the states! Some laws that eventually pass in the U.S. Congress are first considered in small communities across America.

A democracy depends upon its citizens for success. Remember, democracy means "the people rule." Citizens obey laws, educate themselves about the issues, let their representatives know what they think, vote in elections, and participate by volunteering in their communities. Think about your community. Who is a role model of good citizenship? Your state capitol is a symbol of representative democracy and of your state. It belongs to the people.

Enjoy your visit and keep on learning!

Alaska State Capitol

Notes

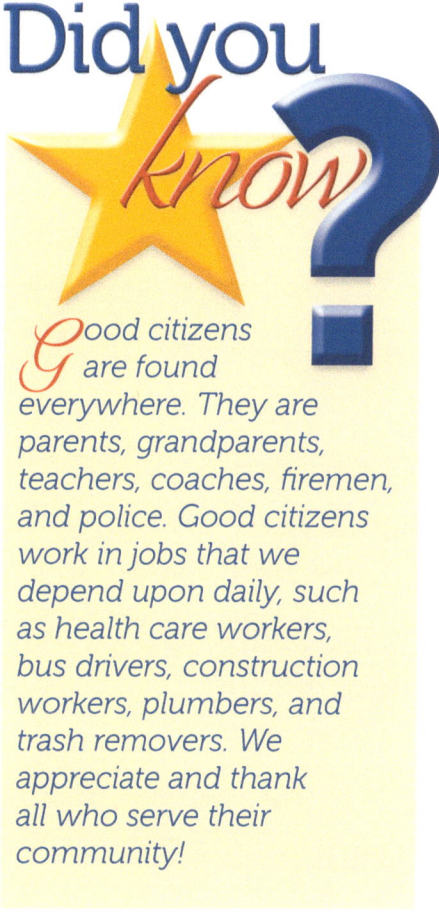

Did you know?

Good citizens are found everywhere. They are parents, grandparents, teachers, coaches, firemen, and police. Good citizens work in jobs that we depend upon daily, such as health care workers, bus drivers, construction workers, plumbers, and trash removers. We appreciate and thank all who serve their community!

Here are some interesting facts about each state capitol. When you visit, look for...

Alabama:
- ★ The beautiful stairways that spiral up to the third floor
- ★ Flags honoring every state found on the capitol grounds

Alaska:
- ★ Murals named "Harvest of the Land" and "Harvest of the Sea" located in the lobby
- ★ Replica of the Liberty Bell given to the territory in 1950

Arizona:
- ★ Arizona history displays in the Old Capitol
- ★ The Old Capitol House and Senate chambers that look as they did in the early 1900s

Arkansas:
- ★ The 4,000-pound chandelier that hangs in the rotunda on a 73-foot chain
- ★ Arkansas limestone used in the interior (inside) of the building

California:
- ★ Landscaped gardens and trees located on the capitol grounds
- ★ State symbols found in the rotunda, including cast iron grizzly bears

Colorado:
- ★ Unique rose onyx marble, not found anywhere else in the world
- ★ Mile-high markers found on the west steps of the capitol

Connecticut:
- ★ The historic Charter Oak Chair
- ★ Twenty-six exterior (outside) statues of famous Connecticut citizens

Delaware:
- ★ Capitol Square complex that includes the Old Capitol and the Legislative Hall
- ★ Legislative Hall interior designed in 18th-century style

Florida:
- ★ The modern skyscraper design of the 22-story capitol building
- ★ The observation deck from which you can view the city of Tallahassee

Georgia:
- Georgia marble (also used in many state capitols) throughout the interior
- Paintings of George Washington and four other American patriots

Hawaii:
- Sun and moon chandeliers in the legislative chambers
- The roofless center section of the capitol that opens to the sky

Idaho:
- Unique sandstone exterior
- Forty-three stars on the interior dome ceiling that tell the story of Idaho statehood

Illinois:
- Stained glass window, State Sovereignty and National Union, at the top of the dome
- "Illinois Welcoming the World," a sculpture of a woman with open arms

Indiana:
- The interior stained glass dome made of 256 panels of colored glass
- Monuments on the grounds that celebrate the history of Indiana

Iowa:
- Four copper domes located on each corner of the capitol
- The mural entitled "Westward" that honors early settlers

Kansas:
- The 22-foot bronze statue of the Kansa warrior Ad Astra that tops the dome
- A statue honoring Abraham Lincoln located on the capitol grounds

Kentucky:
- The grand corridor that features 36 granite columns
- Frontier scenes with Daniel Boone at the entrances to the House and Senate chambers

Louisiana:
- Exterior stone steps that name the states of the union
- Murals found in Memorial Hall that show Louisiana as a land of plenty

Maine:
- The sculpture "The Lady of Wisdom" at the top of the dome
- Dioramas that illustrate wildlife found in Maine

Maryland:
- ★ The room where George Washington met with the Continental Congress in 1783
- ★ An acorn, symbol of strength, found on the top of the cupola

Massachusetts:
- ★ Grounds that include statues of important citizens of Massachusetts
- ★ The "sacred cod" carving that hangs in the House of Representatives chamber

Michigan:
- ★ The floor of the rotunda that is made up of nearly 1,000 pieces of glass
- ★ Original chandeliers in the House and Senate chambers

Minnesota:
- ★ Exterior golden sculpture "The Quadriga" of a four-horse chariot and figures
- ★ The elaborately decorated Governor's Reception Room

Mississippi:
- ★ Magnolia trees (the state tree and flower) found on the capitol grounds
- ★ The blindfolded lady representing justice located at the top of the interior dome

Missouri:
- ★ A monument to the Louisiana Purchase that sits on a bank of the Missouri River
- ★ Stained glass, murals, and statues created by several well-known artists

Montana:
- ★ The statue honoring Jeannette Rankin, the first woman elected to the US Congress
- ★ The Charles Russell painting of the Lewis and Clark expedition in the House chamber

Nebraska:
- ★ A sculpture, "The Sower," found at the top of the dome
- ★ Marble floor mosaic entitled "Earth as the Life-giver" located in the center of the rotunda

Nevada:
- ★ Battle Born Hall, which celebrates Nevada's history
- ★ Octagonal (8-sided) dome topped with a cupola

New Hampshire:
- ★ The statue of Daniel Webster that stands at the entrance to the capitol
- ★ Legislative chambers that are the oldest in the nation still used by a state legislature

New Jersey:
- ★ The brass chandelier in the Assembly, installed by Thomas Edison's electric company
- ★ Murals located in the Senate chamber celebrating freedom and prosperity

New Mexico:
- ★ The Capitol Art Collection displays featuring New Mexican artists
- ★ Stained glass rotunda ceiling skylight patterned after a Native American basket

New York:
- ★ The "Million Dollar Staircase" that includes 77 famous faces carved from sandstone
- ★ Two 6-foot high fireplaces in the Senate chamber that are used as private meeting spaces

North Carolina:
- ★ Rotunda plaques and busts honoring people and events in North Carolina history
- ★ The old legislative chambers designed to resemble a Grecian amphitheater and temple

North Dakota:
- ★ The 19th-floor observation deck that provides views of the city
- ★ Lighting in the House chamber that represent a full moon and stars over a prairie sky

Ohio:
- ★ "Greek Revival" style of architecture based on the buildings of ancient Greece
- ★ The map room that includes a marble and limestone map of all 88 Ohio counties

Oklahoma:
- ★ The color scheme of the dome that represents the state wildflower, the Indian Blanket
- ★ Oil wells surrounding the capitol, including "Petunia #1," drilled in a flower bed

Oregon:
- ★ The gold-covered bronze statue "The Oregon Pioneer" that is found atop the building
- ★ The bronze state seal in center of the rotunda

Pennsylvania:
- ★ The 272-foot dome inspired by St. Peter's Basilica in Rome
- ★ Pennsylvania German folk-art tiles that cover the first floor of the rotunda and other halls

Rhode Island:
★ White Georgia marble that covers the building, including the dome
★ The Rhode Island Charter Museum that showcases the original Royal Charter of 1663

South Carolina:
★ Statue of John C. Calhoun, U.S. vice president, secretary of state, and secretary of war
★ The oldest original mace, which represents the authority of the House, used in the U.S.

South Dakota:
★ The Tree of Life images in the rotunda
★ Original brass door knobs that depict the South Dakota State Seal in the center

Tennessee:
★ Portraits of former governors and three U.S. presidents (Jackson, Polk, and Johnson)
★ Original chandeliers in the house and senate chambers

Texas:
★ The star located at the top of the dome, which is surrounded by the letters T-E-X-A-S
★ Portraits in the legislative chambers of famous Texans, including James Bowie

Utah:
★ Marble lions *Fortitude* and *Integrity* found at the east entrance
★ The Old Murals in the House chamber that tell the story of Brigham Young

Vermont:
★ The statue of Ceres, goddess of agriculture, atop the copper and gold-leaf dome
★ Black walnut desks and chairs first used in 1859 and found in the Senate chamber

Virginia:
★ Thomas Jefferson's original model of the capitol that he sent from France to Richmond
★ The 1796 life-size marble statue of George Washington sculpted by Jean Houdon

Washington:
★ The exterior Winged Victory Monument, honoring those who served in World War I
★ The state seal in the floor of the rotunda, used also on railings, door knobs, and furniture

West Virginia:
- ★ Nine different types of marble found in the interior of the capitol
- ★ The gold eagle atop the dome which has a 3-foot wide base and is 5 feet tall

Wisconsin:
- ★ Four monuments, including one to the state constitution, at the foot of the grand staircase
- ★ Decorative skylights found in the four chambers located on the second floor

Wyoming:
- ★ Eight murals, four in each legislative chamber, that tell the story of Wyoming
- ★ Statues of Chief Washakie and Esther Hobart Morris located at the entrance to the capitol

www.ingramcontent.com/pod-product-compliance
Lightning Source LLC
Chambersburg PA
CBHW042147290426
44110CB00003B/140